The Night Before
the First Christmas
Shelly Clarkson

ISBN 979-8-89043-374-9 (paperback)
ISBN 979-8-89043-375-6 (hardcover)
ISBN 979-8-89043-376-3 (digital)

Christian Faith Publishing
832 Park Avenue
Meadville, PA 16335
www.christianfaithpublishing.com

Printed in the United States of America

Acknowledgments

My God, my God, your timing and guidance is amazing.

Mom, Dad, Bubba, Kim, Sam, and the rest of my family, thank you for the support in my darkest times.

Tyler and Paisley, you are the ones that make my world turn. Thank you for your support while working on my book.

My mother-in-law is better than yours. I know that my family and friends are looking down at me, smiling, and proud of this journey.

In loving memory of my sweet friend, Jane Solomon, who pushed me to keep going.

'Twas the night before the first Christmas, and all throughout Bethlehem, every innkeeper was stirring, even their wives and children. The orders were made by Agustus himself to keep count of the people who served him throughout.

The animals were settled, all snug in the hay, while visions of green grass danced in their heads. Mary was with child; and I, a nervous wreck, had just arrived at the end of our very long trek when, in front of the inn, I began to make a clatter. The innkeeper sprang to the door to see what was the matter. Away to the stable he escorted us quickly 'cause Mary was in labor and feeling quite sickly.

The star shone from above on the freshly laid hay and gave a signal to the wise men that the King was on His way.

Then what to my wondering ears should I hear but a chorus of angels singing, "Noel," with a message for the shepherds out in the fields: "A new King is coming, so have no fear."

So they traveled to see Him and praised His
great name
"Praise Jesus! Praise Savior! Praise Teacher and
Master!"
"Praise Immanuel! Praise the Messiah! Praise
Christ and the I Am!"

To the top of the roof and the mountains afar now spread the good new to one and the good news to all. The news of the new King spread to the wise men afar, who knew it was the Messiah by one special star. So up on the camels' backs they flew with their packs full of gifts and frankincense too.

And then in the silence, I heard in the street the pitter-patter of curious feet. As the angels sang and the star shone above, I knew this was the Son of God, sent to show us how to love.

He was swaddled in cloths to keep Him warm, and while He slept, the world seemed so calm. The weight of the world was what He would carry on His back, but for now He was just a babe, and understanding was what we all lacked. His eyes, how they sparkled. His heart, how pure. His life was a gift, and death would be the cure. His hands were so tiny. I wondered if He knew how much He would someday hold, and the glow from the manger was a sight to behold.

The animals in the stable lulled Him to sleep, and the light encircled His head like a wreath. He had a chorus of angels that sang all around Him that spread the great news like trumpets were sounding.

He was tiny yet mighty, a treasure to the world, and I cried when I saw Him 'cause He would change the world. A wrap of some swaddling clothes and a manger of hay were a humble beginning for the King that day. He cried not ever once but gave peace to everyone.

We would stay a few weeks and then flee to Egypt. The wise men would come and tell of a plan. Other kings feared the power that was to come to the land. But they could not stop Him from teaching the good news. But for that night, a new baby would sleep, and how were we to fully know what God had planned on that night?

Bethlehem

HOME
SWEET
HOME

This is Joseph's story of the first Christmas so we
can share with all and to all shine His light.

About the Author

Shelly was gifted by God with a sense of creativity in many areas. Shelly loves to bake and decorate cakes and cookies as well as paint with watercolors and acrylics, and now she's beginning her journey with children's books.

She grew up and graduated in the small town of Mineral Wells, Texas. From birth she was a member of the First United Methodist Church but also attended the Baptist church and South Side Church of Christ on occasion. After she graduated high school in 2003, she moved to Denton, where she would receive a bachelor's degree in child development and a master of science degree in occupational therapy in just five years from the prestigious Texas Women's University. She moved several times after that, including to Norman, Fort Worth, and Wichita Falls, where she had her first professional job placement and her longest so far—at the North Texas Rehab Center.

Shelly currently resides in the Sherman-Denison area, where she worked for another not-for-profit outpatient clinic like the one in Wichita Falls, and she currently works at a skilled nursing facility. Shelly currently attends church at the Parkside Baptist Church with her husband of five years Tyler, their four-year-old daughter Paisley, and her mother-in-law, Donna.

The greatest gift of all.